THE BENE

TO

A HAPPY

LIFE

Imam Abdur Rahman b. Nasir
al-Sa'di (d. 1376H)

Translation Hassan Hussein Abdi

First Edition: 1444H/December 2022CE

Translation: Hassan Hussein Abdi
Reviewed and Edited: Hikmah Publications
Ḥikmah Publications
ISBN: 978-1-7923-6983-4

Address:
Ḥikmah Publications
P.O. Box 44121
Philadelphia, PA. 19144
hikmahpubs@gmail.com

Table of Contents

In the Name of Allah, The Most Merciful, The Bestower of Mercy

[Introduction][1]

All praise belongs to Allah, Who is worthy of all praise. I testify that none has the right to be worshipped in truth except Allah, alone without any partners; and I testify that Muhammad is His slave and Messenger. May Allah's peace and blessings be upon him, his family and his Companions.

To proceed:

Verily, the heart's comfort, serenity and happiness, and the banishment of anxiety and sorrow is the goal of every individual. This is the way to attain a happy life and to achieve joy and delight.

There are religious, natural and practical means to accomplish this. It is not possible for all of these means to collectively be attained except for the believers.

As for anyone else, even though they may attain a share of this happiness from a particular angle or due to a given means, which the intellectuals from among them focus upon, they still miss out on aspects of happiness that are more beneficial and permanent, and more effective in the short-term and long-term.

[1] **[TN]** All headings in brackets have been added by the translator.

In this treatise of mine, I will mention some of the means that come to mind for this ultimate goal, which everyone strives to attain. Some people implement many of them, and thus experience a wonderful existence and live a happy life. Some fail to implement any of them, and thus experience a miserable existence and live a wretched life. Others are somewhere in between, depending on their success in implementing these means.

Allah alone grants success, and His aid alone is sought to attain all that is good and repel all that is evil.[1]

[1] **[TN]** Imam Sa'di wrote this treatise after he was gifted a book of a non-Muslim discussing happiness and the relief of worry and stress, while he was in hospital in Beirut. Shaykh Ibn 'Uthaymin mentioned that after Imam Sa'di read the book he said, "This book has many benefits, but it was written by a non-Muslim, so he failed to discuss a number of important fundamentals connected to happiness."

Chapter

[Faith and Righteous Deeds]

Faith and righteous deeds are the greatest means to achieve a happy life, and they are the foundation and basis of this.

Allah, the Most High said:

مَنْ عَمِلَ صَٰلِحًا مِّن ذَكَرٍ أَوْ أُنثَىٰ وَهُوَ مُؤْمِنٌ فَلَنُحْيِيَنَّهُۥ حَيَوٰةً
طَيِّبَةً ۖ وَلَنَجْزِيَنَّهُمْ أَجْرَهُم بِأَحْسَنِ مَا كَانُوا۟ يَعْمَلُونَ

> "Whoever works righteousness, whether male or female, while they are a believer, We will surely give them a good life, and We shall certainly reward them according to the best of what they used to do." [Al-Nahl: 97]

Allah informed us, and promised, that whoever combines faith and righteous deeds, then He will give them a good life in this world and a tremendous reward in this world and in the Hereafter.

The reason behind this is clear. Those who believe in Allah with correct belief, which results in righteous deeds and rectifies the hearts, the character and [the affairs of] this life and the Hereafter, possess foundations and fundamentals to deal with events of happiness and delight, and to cope with the events of worry, anxiety and sadness.

Therefore, they receive moments of happiness and joy with acceptance and gratitude, and they utilize them for that which is beneficial. When they approach them in this manner it results in more delight, a desire for them to remain and be further blessed, and a hope to attain the reward of the thankful. These are amazing things that surpass, along with their good and blessings, the original pleasures, which these fruits stem from.

Conversely, they encounter difficulties, hardships, anxiety and sorrow by repelling whatever can be resisted, lessening whatever can be minimized and showing beautiful patience in the face of whatever they are unable to escape. As a result of the consequences of these difficulties – the beneficial struggles, the experiences, the strength, the patience and awaiting the reward and recompense – they achieve great things that make light of these difficulties and replace them with joy, good aspirations and fervent desire for Allah's favor and reward.

The Prophet (peace and blessings be upon him) expressed this in the authentic *Hadith* where he said:

عَجَبًا لأَمْرِ الْمُؤْمِنِ إِنَّ أَمْرَهُ كُلَّهُ خَيْرٌ إِنْ أَصَابَتْهُ سَرَّاءُ شَكَرَ فَكَانَ خَيْرًا لَهُ
وَإِنْ أَصَابَتْهُ ضَرَّاءُ صَبرَ فَكَانَ خَيْرًا لَهُ وَلَيْسَ ذَلِكَ لأَحَدٍ إِلاَّ لِلْمُؤْمِنِ

> "Amazing is the affair of the believer, as all his affairs are good. If prosperity touches him, he is grateful, and that is better for him; and if hardship befalls him, he is patient, and that is better for him. This is exclusively for the believer."[1]

The Prophet (peace and blessings be upon him) informed us that the believer's rewards, good and fruits of his righteous deeds multiply every time he experiences pleasure and difficulties. This is why oftentimes you will find two people who experience the same fluctuations of good and evil, but they differ vastly in the way they deal with them, according to the levels of their faith and righteous deeds.

The one who possesses these two attributes [i.e. faith and righteous deeds] responds to good and bad with gratitude and patience, as we mentioned. This brings him happiness and delight, and it results in the elimination of anxiety, sorrow, distress, unhappiness and misery of life; and he lives a happy life in this world.

The other person [who lacks these qualities] responds to blessings and pleasant things with insolence, arrogance and transgression, and thus his mannerisms further deteriorate, and he receives them like an animal with greed and restlessness. Despite this, his heart is still not content, rather it is anxious for a number of reasons. He is anxious because he fears the loss of the things that he loves, and due to the many

[1] Muslim (no. 2999).

struggles normally associated with them. He is also anxious because the souls are endlessly desirous, and they continuously covet more things, which he may or may not acquire. Even if he acquired them – assuming that this is the case – then he would still be perturbed due to the aforementioned reasons.

As for difficulties, then such a person encounters them with unease, anxiety, fear and irritation. Do not even ask about the misery it causes in their life, and the resulting psychological and mental illnesses; and the fear that develops, which could reach the most horrid levels and lead to the most abhorred discomforts. This is because he neither hopes for a reward nor does he have any patience to comfort him and lighten this affliction.

All of this is visible and known through experience. There is one example of this, if you were to reflect upon it and apply it to the conditions of humankind, then you would see the great difference between the believer who acts upon the requisites of his faith and the one who is opposite to this. [The reason is that] the religion strongly encourages to be content with the sustenance of Allah and with that which He bestows upon the servants from His grace and various favors.

So, the believer, if tested with sickness, poverty or a similar trial that everyone is subjected to, then due to his faith, his contentment and satisfaction with what Allah has apportioned for him, you find him gratified. His heart does not seek an affair that has not been destined for him. He looks at those less fortunate, and he does not look at those above him. His joy, happiness and serenity might surpass someone who has all the worldly pleasures, if they have not been blessed with contentment.

Similarly, you find the one who does not act upon the requisites of faith, if tested with poverty or the loss of some worldly pleasures, then you find him in utter misery and distress.

Another example is when fearful things occur, and disturbing events befall a person, you find the one with strong faith having a firm heart and a serene soul. Therefore, they can govern and steer the affair that has unexpectedly afflicted them through thought, speech and action that is within their ability. They have prepared themselves for this disturbing calamity. These are responses that put a person at ease and strengthen their heart.

However, you find the one lacking faith is the total opposite under such circumstances. When fearful events arise, his heart is perturbed, his nerves become tense, his thoughts are scattered, and fear and terror seize him. He suffers from both external fear and internal restlessness, the true nature of which cannot be described.

This type of person, if they do not have some natural means [to resist these difficulties], which requires much training, then their strength is depleted, and their nerves are jittery and on edge. This is because of the absence of faith, which prompts patience, especially in difficult times and disturbing and upsetting circumstances.

The pious and impious, and the believer and disbeliever, both share in the ability to attain acquired courage, and to develop the instinct to lighten and ease these fear-provoking situations. However, the believer is distinct due to his strength of faith, patience, reliance upon Allah, dependence upon Him, and his desire for Allah's reward. These are qualities that make him more courageous, reduce for him the agony of fear and ease him of [the burden of] these difficulties.

As Allah, the Most High said:

إِن تَكُونُوا۟ تَأْلَمُونَ فَإِنَّهُمْ يَأْلَمُونَ كَمَا تَأْلَمُونَ ۖ وَتَرْجُونَ مِنَ ٱللَّهِ مَا لَا يَرْجُونَ ۗ

> "If you are suffering, then surely they are suffering as you are suffering, but you hope to receive from Allah that which they hope not." [Al-Nisa: 104]

They also receive Allah's aid, specific *Ma'iyyah* [With-ness] and help that will banish such frightful situations.

Allah, the Blessed and Most High said:

وَٱصْبِرُوٓا۟ ۚ إِنَّ ٱللَّهَ مَعَ ٱلصَّـٰبِرِينَ

"And be patient. Indeed, Allah is with the patient." [Al-Anfal: 46]

[Benevolence Towards the Creation]

From the means to banish anxiety, sorrow and worry is benevolence to the creation through speech, actions and the types of good treatment, as all of them are good and [acts of] benevolence. By way of this, Allah removes anxieties and sorrows from the pious and the wicked, depending upon the degree of this [benevolence and good treatment].

However, the believer has the most complete share and portion of this. He is distinguished in this regard because his benevolence stems from sincerity and a desire for Allah's reward. As a result, Allah makes it easy for him to generously do good acts, and He repels from him difficulties, due to his sincerity and seeking Allah's reward.

Allah, the Blessed and Most High said:

لَّا خَيْرَ فِي كَثِيرٍ مِّن نَّجْوَىٰهُمْ إِلَّا مَنْ أَمَرَ بِصَدَقَةٍ أَوْ مَعْرُوفٍ أَوْ
إِصْلَٰحٍ بَيْنَ ٱلنَّاسِ ۚ وَمَن يَفْعَلْ ذَٰلِكَ ٱبْتِغَآءَ مَرْضَاتِ ٱللَّهِ فَسَوْفَ
نُؤْتِيهِ أَجْرًا عَظِيمًا

> "There is no good in most of their secret talks, except those who encourage charity, good acts, or reconciliation between the people. And whoever does this, seeking Allah's Pleasure, We shall give him a great reward." [Al-Nisa: 114]

He, the Blessed and Most High, informed us that all of these things [mentioned in the verse] are good deeds for those who perform them, and good brings good and repels evil; and that Allah will give the believer who desires His reward a great recompense. The elimination of anxiety, sorrow, anguish and anything similar is part of this reward.

Chapter

[Occupying Oneself with Beneficial Knowledge or Actions]

From the means to repel anxiety, which stems from nervousness and the heart being preoccupied with troublesome thoughts, is occupying oneself with an action or type of beneficial knowledge.

This will distract the heart from preoccupying itself with the the matter that is troubling it. It may also make it forget about the things that have caused it anxiety and sorrow, so his soul becomes happy and his zeal increases.

This is also something that is applicable to the believer and disbeliever. However, the believer is distinct due to his faith, sincerity and seeking Allah's pleasure when he busies himself with the knowledge that he is learning or a good action he is performing. [This is true] whether it is an act of worship, in which case it is considered to be religious worship, a worldly activity, or practice accompanied by a righteous intention and intended to aid in the obedience of Allah. For this reason, it has a powerful effect in removing anxieties, sorrows and miseries.

How many people have been afflicted with distress and constant worries, which results in them suffering from various illnesses? Thus, the effective cure for them is to forget the reason that caused this distress and worry, and for them to preoccupy themselves with an action from their daily activities.

This activity that he busies himself with must be something that the soul enjoys and yearns for, as this surely will have a more thorough effect in actualizing this beneficial goal. And Allah knows best.

[Occupying Oneself with the Present]

From the things that repel anxiety and misery is absolute focus in concentrating on the actions of the present day, and not worrying about the future, nor being sad about the past.

This is why the Prophet (peace and blessings be upon him) sought refuge with Allah from anxiety and grief. Grief is connected to past events that cannot be prevented nor altered. Anxiety stems from fear about the future.

Therefore, the servant should be a person who focuses on his present day, exerting his effort and determination to better his day and present state. Focusing the heart on this results in the completion of one's actions, and it provides solace to the servant, freeing him of anxiety and grief.

When the Prophet (peace and blessings be upon him) supplicated to Allah with a supplication or directed his nation to a supplication, he encouraged them to exert effort and determination – along with seeking the aid of Allah and desiring His favor – to successfully attain what they are supplicating for and to escape what they are asking to be removed. This is because supplication is paired with actions.

The servant strives for that which will benefit his religion and worldly affairs and asks his Lord for the fruition of his aspirations, seeking His aid in that. As he (peace and blessings be upon him) said:

احْرِصْ عَلَى مَا يَنْفَعُكَ، وَاسْتَعِنْ بِاللَّهِ وَلَا تَعْجِزْ، وَإِنْ أَصَابَكَ شَيْءٌ فَلَا تَقُلْ: لَوْ أَنِّي فَعَلْتُ كَانَ كَذَا وَكَذَا. وَلَكِنْ قُلْ: قَدَرُ اللَّهِ وَمَا شَاءَ فَعَلَ. فَإِنَّ لَوْ تَفْتَحُ عَمَلَ الشَّيْطَانِ

> "Strive for that which will benefit you and seek the aid of Allah; and do not be lazy. If something afflicts you, do not say, 'If I had done such and such, then such and such would have happened.' Rather say, 'This is the Decree of Allah, and He does what He wills,' as 'if' opens [an entrance] for the Devil's work."[1]

He (peace and blessings be upon him) combined the command to strive for beneficial things in all circumstances, to seek the aid of Allah and to not surrender to laziness (harmful idleness), with acceptance of past occurrences and acknowledgment of Allah's Divine Decree and Preordainment.

He divided these affairs into two categories:

The first category are those things that the slave is able to achieve completely or partially, or repel completely or partially. The servant should strive his utmost to achieve this while seeking the aid of his Lord Whom he worships.

[1] Muslim (2664).

The second category are those things that cannot be accomplished. The servant must be content with this, pleased and submissive.

There is no doubt that conforming to this fundamental principle is a reason for happiness and the elimination of anxiety and distress.

Chapter

[Remembering Allah Often]

Among the greatest reasons for the happiness of the heart and its serenity is much remembrance of Allah, as this has a remarkable effect in bringing about the happiness of the heart and its serenity, and the elimination of anxiety and grief. He, the Blessed and Most High said:

أَلَا بِذِكْرِ ٱللَّهِ تَطْمَئِنُّ ٱلْقُلُوبُ

> "Surely in the remembrance of Allah the hearts find comfort." [Al-Ra'd: 28]

The remembrance of Allah has a profound effect in the attainment of this desired objective due to its uniqueness, and due to the servant hoping for the reward and recompense of Allah.

[Acknowledging Allah's Blessings]

Another thing is mentioning Allah's blessings, the apparent and the hidden. Acknowledging and mentioning them is a reason for Allah to remove anxiety and distress from the servant, which causes him to be thankful. This is the highest and loftiest station, even if the servant is in a state of poverty, sickness or any other type of calamity.

When the servant compares the blessings of Allah upon him, which cannot be counted nor calculated, with the afflictions that befall him, then the afflictions are negligible in comparison.

In reality, when the servant is tested with trials and tribulations, and he observes the necessary patience, contentment and submission, then their burden is lightened, and their difficulty is alleviated. Furthermore, the servant's hope to earn the anticipated reward and recompense for these trials and his servitude to Allah through patience and contentment transforms bitterness into sweetness. Thus, the sweetness of the reward causes him to forget about the bitterness of patience [upon that trial].

[Looking at Those Less Fortunate Than You]

Among the most effective means in this regard is to implement the instructions of the Prophet (peace and blessings be upon him), which he referred to in the authentic *Hadith*:

> "Look at those who are below you, and do not look at those who are above you, as surely this will assist you to not belittle the blessings of Allah upon you."[1]

When the servant places these honorable teachings before his eyes, he will definitely see that he has surpassed many of the creation in wellbeing and associated matters, and in terms of sustenance and connected matters, regardless of his situation. Thus, his misery, anxiety and worry disappear, and his happiness and delight with the blessings of Allah, through which he surpasses others who are below him, increase.

The more the servant reflects over the apparent and hidden religious and worldly blessings that Allah has bestowed upon him, then he will appreciate that his Lord has given him much good, and He has protected him from various types of evils.

[1] Bukhari (6490) Muslim (2963).

There is no doubt that this removes anxiety and worry and results in happiness and joy.

[Eliminating the Causes of Anxiety]

Among the decisive means that result in happiness and the removal of anxiety and worry is striving to eliminate the causes of anxiety and to attain the means that bring about happiness.

This is attained by forgetting about the past misfortunes that cannot be averted nor altered, and by understanding that overthinking about these things is foolish and pointless. It is actually stupidity and insanity.

He must struggle against his heart to prevent it from thinking about these affairs. He must also struggle against his heart to prevent it from worrying about what he foresees for the future like poverty, fear and other afflictions, which he imagines will befall him in the future.

He should know that the outcomes of the future are unknown, whether good or bad, or hopes or pains; he should know that all of this in the Hand of the All-Mighty, the All-Wise. The servant has no control over any of this, and the only thing he can do is strive to attain the good and repel the evil.

The servant should know that when he stops his mind from worrying about the future, and instead relies upon his Lord to rectify these affairs and trusts Him concerning this; when he does this, his heart will be content, his affairs will be in order and his anxiety and worry will vanish.

[Supplication of the Prophet]

Among the most effective means to prepare for future affairs is implementing the supplication that the Prophet (peace and blessings be upon him) used to say:

اللَّهُمَّ أَصْلِحْ لِي دِينِي الَّذِي هُوَ عِصْمَةُ أَمْرِي، وَأَصْلِحْ لِي دُنْيَايَ الَّتِي فِيهَا مَعَاشِي، وَأَصْلِحْ لِي آخِرَتِي الَّتِي فِيهَا مَعَادِي، وَاجْعَلِ الْحَيَاةَ زِيَادَةً لِي فِي كُلِّ خَيْرٍ، وَاجْعَلِ الْمَوْتَ رَاحَةً لِي مِنْ كُلِّ شَرٍّ

"O Allah, rectify my religion which is the safeguard of all my affairs, rectify for me my worldly affairs in which is my livelihood, and rectify for me my Hereafter which is my afterlife. Make life a further means for me for all that is good and death an alleviation from all that is evil."[1]

Similarly, his (peace blessings be upon him) saying:

اللَّهُمَّ رَحْمَتَكَ أَرْجُو، فَلَا تَكِلْنِي إِلَى نَفْسِي طَرْفَةَ عَيْنٍ، وَأَصْلِحْ لِي شَأْنِي كُلَّهُ، لَا إِلَهَ إِلَّا أَنْتَ

[1] Muslim (2720).

> "O Allah, it is only Your mercy I hope for, so do not leave me to myself for the blinking of an eye. Rectify all of my affairs; none has the right to be worshipped but You."[1]

If the servant continually calls upon Allah with this supplication, which comprises of the rectification of his future religious and worldly affairs, with an attentive heart and a sincere intention while striving to attain this, then Allah will grant him what he has asked, hoped for and acted to accomplish; and his anxiety will transform into happiness and joy.

[1] **Hasan.** Abu Dawud (5090).

Chapter

[Expecting the Worst]

One of the most beneficial ways to eliminate worry and anxiety when calamities befall a servant is to strive to lessen their effect by expecting the worst possible outcome and preparing oneself for that. If he does this, then he should strive to lighten this as much as he is able. By this preparation and this beneficial striving, his anxiety and worries disappear, and the consequence of this is that striving to bring about benefit and ward off harm is made easy for the servant.

If the servant is afflicted with things that cause fear, sicknesses, poverty and the loss of things beloved to him, then let him encounter these trials with calmness and by preparing the soul for that; rather, for the worst imaginable scenario.

Verily, preparing the soul to endure these afflictions eases their burden and removes any associated distress, especially if he preoccupies himself with attempting to resist them according to his ability.

Thus, he combines preparation of the soul along with constructive effort, which will distract him from absorbing himself in these calamities; and he struggles against his soul to renew his strength to resist these hardships, while depending upon Allah and completely trusting Him.

There is no doubt that these affairs have great benefit in attaining happiness and pleasure, in addition to the reward that the servant anticipates in this life and the next.

This has been tried and tested, and there are accounts of many people who have experienced this.

[Strength of Heart]

One of the best cures for anxiety disorders of the heart, and even for the illnesses of the body, is fortitude of the heart and it not being disturbed and troubled by delusions and paranoia, which stem from bad thoughts.

This is because when a person surrenders to delusions and his heart is disturbed by the effects of fear, illness, anger, and confusion due to painful triggers – and anticipation of calamities and the expectation of losing coveted things – then this will cause him to sink into anxiety, depression, disorders of the heart and body, and a nervous breakdown, which has horrid consequences. The people have witnessed the many harms of this.

[Reliance Upon Allah]

When the heart depends upon Allah, truly relies upon Him and does not succumb to illusions nor controlled by evil thoughts, while trusting in Allah and desiring His favor, then anxiety and sorrow will quickly disappear from it. Many mental and physical disorders will be alleviated. Furthermore, the heart will acquire inner strength, happiness and joy, above and beyond that which can be described.

How many hospitals are full of sick people who suffer from schizophrenia and paranoid delusions! How much has this troubled the hearts of the strong, let alone the weak! How many times has this led to feeble-mindedness and insanity!

The only one who is saved from this is the person that Allah safeguards with wellbeing and grants him success to strive against his soul to attain the beneficial means that will strengthen his heart and repel misery from it.

Allah said:

وَمَن يَتَوَكَّلْ عَلَى ٱللَّهِ فَهُوَ حَسْبُهُۥٓ

> "Whosoever puts his trust in Allah, then He is sufficient for him." [Al-Talaq: 3]

This means that Allah will suffice him in everything that concerns him as it relates to his religion and worldly affairs. The one who places his trust in Allah possesses a strong heart and is not affected by delusive thoughts nor disturbed by unexpected events. This is because he knows that this stems from weakness of the soul and feebleness and fear, which has no reality.

Furthermore, he knows that Allah has promised to fully suffice those who rely upon Him. Therefore, he trusts Allah and is certain of His promise, so his anxiety and worry vanish, and his difficulty is replaced with ease, his grief by delight and his fear by peace.

We ask Allah, the Blessed and Most High, for wellbeing, and to grace us with firmness and strength of the heart through absolute reliance in Him, as Allah has promised such a person with all that is good and to protect him from all that is evil and harmful.

Chapter

[Overlooking the Shortcomings of the People]

There are two tremendous benefits in the saying of the Prophet (peace and blessings be upon him):

لَا يَفْرَكْ مُؤْمِنٌ مُؤْمِنَةً إِنْ كَرِهَ مِنْهَا خُلُقًا رَضِيَ مِنْهَا آخَرَ

> "A believing man should not despise a believing woman. If he dislikes one of her characteristics, then he is pleased by another."[1]

Firstly, it contains guidance on how to deal with the wife, relative, friend, colleague and anyone you have a connection or interaction with, and that you must train yourself to expect from them deficiencies, shortcomings and things that you dislike.

If you find any of the aforementioned, then you should take into consideration what is obligatory upon you, or appropriate for you to do, as it relates to the importance of this relationship, preserving the ties of love, remembering the commendable qualities and the overall objectives, specific and general.

[1] Muslim (1469).

By overlooking these shortcomings and focusing on the good qualities, friendships and relationships last, and harmony is achieved. It will also result in you attaining the second benefit [found in this *Hadith*], which is the elimination of anxiety and worry, the continuation of sincere friendship, the fulfilment of rights and responsibilities, whether obligatory or recommended, and the establishment of a harmonious relationship between the two parties.

Whoever fails to adhere to this advice mentioned by the Prophet (peace and blessings be upon him), and instead does the opposite by focusing on the shortcomings whilst being blind about the good qualities, will surely be miserable; and they will ruin any love between themselves and those whom they have relationships with, and they will neglect many of the rights that they both must preserve and fulfill.

Many of the people who are known for their resolve and strong determination adequately prepare themselves to endure calamities and tragedies with patience and calmness. However, they behave irrationally and ruin relationships for the most petty and trivial matters.

The reason for this behavior is that they prepared themselves for major trials and tests, but were careless in the face of minor ones, and thus it disturbed and harmed their tranquility.

The resolute, wise individual prepares himself for major and minor issues, and asks Allah for His aid and to not leave him to his own devices for the blinking of an eye. This is how minor problems will be easy for him to deal with just like major ones, and he will remain at ease with a tranquil soul and serene heart.

Chapter

[Life Is Short; Cherish the Happy Moments]

The intelligent person knows that real life is the life lived in happiness and tranquility, and that this life is very short. Therefore, he should not make it even shorter with anxiety and endless worries. This contradicts a meaningful existence. Let him be tenaciously stingy with his life and not allow large portions of it to be robbed from him by anxieties and worries.

This is applicable to the righteous and the wicked; however, the believer has the greatest share of this and the beneficial portion in this life and the next.

[Remembering the Blessings]

Similarly, when an adversity afflicts him, or he fears one, he should compare this difficulty to the existing religious and worldly blessings. This evaluation will highlight the abundant blessings he presently enjoys and the insignificance of the affliction.

He should likewise evaluate the harm that he fears will affect him considering the many possibilities to escape it. Thus, he should not allow a weak possibility to overcome numerous strong possibilities. This will result in his anxiety and fear disappearing.

He should expect for the worst possibility to befall him, and he should prepare himself for that, if it occurs; and he should try and repel what has yet to occur, and to remove or lessen what has already occurred.

[Ignoring the Attacks of the People]

One of the beneficial things is to know that the harm of the people cannot hurt you, especially as it relates to evil speech. It only harms them, unless you concern yourself with it and allow it to influence your feelings. In that case, it will harm you, as it harmed them. If you pay no attention to it, then it will not harm you in the slightest.

[Your Life Is Dependent Upon Your Thoughts]

Know that your life is dependent on your thoughts. So, if your thoughts revolve around things that will benefit you in your religion or worldly affairs, then your life will be pleasant and happy. The opposite is also true.

[Do Not Expect Thanks from the People]

Among the most effective ways to repel depression is to accustom yourself to not expect appreciation except from Allah. If you treat someone who has a right upon you or no such right benevolently, then know that this is due to your good etiquettes with Allah, so do not worry about being thanked by them.

Allah said about the best of His creation:

إِنَّمَا نُطْعِمُكُمْ لِوَجْهِ ٱللَّهِ لَا نُرِيدُ مِنكُمْ جَزَآءً وَلَا شُكُورًا

> "We feed you only seeking the Face of Allah. We desire not from you reward nor gratitude." [Al-Insan: 9]

This is further stressed when dealing with one's family, children and anyone you have strong relations with. So when you prepare yourself to refrain from censuring them when they do not show thanks[1], then you bring peace to yourself and are at ease.

---

[1] **[TN]** This appears to be the intent of the author, and Allah knows best. Refer to the explanation of this treatise printed by *Al-Ubaykan*, p. 47.

[Engaging In the Best of Things]

Among the reasons of tranquility is to focus on virtuous qualities, and to work towards them and implement them according to one's inner drive, without overexertion. Overexertion results in stress and in you turning back on your heels empty-handed without this noble objective. This is because you traversed upon a crooked path.

It is from wisdom that you extract something pleasant and pure from something disturbing and grim. This increases the enjoyment of pleasant moments and eliminates sorrow.

Focus on beneficial things and work to complete them, and do not concern yourself with detrimental things in order to distract you from the sources of your anxiety and sorrow.

Take advantage of times of ease and relaxation to complete important tasks.

[Completing Current Responsibilities]

Among the beneficial means is to finish tasks immediately and free up one's time for future tasks. This is because if actions are left incomplete, then they pile up along with the previous ones, and they are added to any future work. As a result, the pressure becomes even greater. When you complete everything at its appropriate time, then you can face future responsibilities with strength of mind and vigor.

[Give Priority to Important Duties]

You should choose beneficial actions according to their priority, starting with the most important. Differentiate between what your soul likes and strongly desires [and what it does not.] This is because the opposite will result in boredom, apathy and distress.

Utilize in this regard your precise deliberation and consultation, as the one who consults others will never regret [his decision].

Study carefully what you intend to do. If you are certain about its benefit and resolute to proceed, then place your trust in Allah, as Allah loves those who place their trust in Him.

This is the conclusion of this treatise.

And all praise belongs to Allah, the Lord of all the creation; and may peace and blessings be upon our leader, Muhammad and his Companions.

Made in the USA
Middletown, DE
09 January 2023

21761910R00024